Year 5

Fiction & Poetry Writing

by Heather Bell

Introduction

Photocopiable Fiction and Poetry Writing for Year 5 is designed as an aid to the busy classroom teacher planning extended writing activities for the Literacy Strategy.

The objectives for each activity are taken directly from the National Literacy Strategy.

The author has chosen a selection of passages from different genre by leading children's writers, in the belief that good literature 'speaks' and is an excellent stimulus for writing.

Writing frames are included, to aid children when they are planning their writing. For those children who struggle to think up ideas, or who have special needs, there are writing support sheets for many of the activities.

Topical Resources, P.O. Box 329,
Broughton,
Preston,
Lancashire.
PR3 5LT

Topical Resources publishes a range of Educational Materials for use in Primary Schools and Pre-School Nurseries and Playgroups.

For the latest catalogue
Tel 01772 863158
Fax 01772 866153
e.mail:sales@topical-resources.co.uk
Visit our Website at:
www.topical-resources.co.uk

Illustrated by John Hutchinson & Paul Sealey

Typeset by Paul Sealey Illustration & Design,
3 Wentworth Drive, Thornton, Lancashire.

Printed in Great Britain for 'Topical Resources', Publishers of Educational Materials, P.O. Box 329, Broughton, Preston, Lancashire PR3 5LT by T.Snape & Company Limited, Boltons Court, Preston Lancashire.

First Published January 2002

ISBN 1 872977 63 4

Acknowledgments

The author and publishers would like to thank the following for permission to use these extracts:

'Tom's Midnight Garden' by Philippa Pearce, by permission of Oxford University Press.

'Breathless' from 'South Col' by Wilfred Noyce, published by Heinemann. Used by permission of The Random House Group Limited.

'How the Whale Became' by Ted Hughes with permission of Faber and Faber Ltd.

'Chivvy' by Michael Rosen. Reprinted by permission of PFD on behalf of Michael Rosen.

'Moses the Kitten' by James Herriot. Publishers Michael Joseph by kind permission of David Higham Associates.

'The Birth of Jesus' & 'The Good Samaritan' quoted from Good News Bible published by The Bible Societies / Harper Collins Publishers Ltd. UK. © American Bible Society, 1966, 1971, 1976, 1992.

The publishers have endeavoured to trace the copyright holders of all the texts in this publication. If we have unwittingly infringed copyright, we sincerely apologise and will be pleased, on being satisfied as to the owner's title, to pay an appropriate fee as if we had been able to obtain prior permission.

Contents

Reading Response Sheet

Teacher's Notes

Reading Response Sheet

National Literacy Strategy Y5 Term 1:

To record their ideas, reflections and predictions about a book, for example, through a reading log or journal.

The children should be given a copy of the photocopiable Reading Response Sheet to complete when they are part way through reading a book. It will encourage the children to clarify their personal response to a text and to record this in a coherent manner. The children should complete the final section of the Reading Response Sheet after they have finished the story. It will be interesting for them to compare their prediction of what they thought might happen, to what actually happens in the story.

The Reading Response Sheets could then be filed in a class Reading Response Book. The children could be encouraged to look at their peer's responses prior to choosing a new book from the class library. Some children tend to 'get hooked' on an author and do not broaden their range. This activity is a useful way of overcoming this problem. The Reading Response file would be best displayed in a prominent and accessible place in the classroom.

Reading Response Sheet

Writing Frame

Name: ______________________ **Date:** ____________

Reading Response sheet.. ....

Book title ....

By ....

A summary of what has happened in the story so far:

The main characters in the story are ______________________

I liked/ disliked ______________________ because

The part of the story I have enjoyed most is:

What I think will happen next in the story is:

Was I right in my prediction? (Complete this after you have finished reading the story).

Sleeping Beauty

The fairies were once asked to the christening of a baby princess. One fairy was not invited, so she cast an evil spell on to the child. She said that on the girl's eighteenth birthday she would prick her finger on a spinning wheel and die.

However, a good fairy cast another spell to say that the princess would not die, but sleep for 100 years. She could only be awakened by a kiss.

The princess grew up to be beautiful and good. On her 18th birthday, she went to a room high up in the castle and found an old lady spinning. (This was the bad fairy in disguise.) The princess touched the spindle and fell asleep. Soon the whole palace fell asleep exactly where they were.

Time went by. The hedge around the palace grew thicker and thicker. One day a handsome prince came riding by. He went to explore. He cut back the hedge and found the palace. He went into the palace and found the room where the princess lay asleep.

He kissed her and immediately everyone inside the palace awoke after the long sleep. The prince and princess married and lived happily ever after.

Teacher's Notes

National Literacy Strategy Y5 Term 1:

To map out texts showing development and structure eg. Its high and low points, the links between sections, paragraphs, chapters.

Ensure firstly that the children are familiar with the story of Sleeping Beauty. It may be useful to read this to them to refresh their memories of the sequence of events.

Explain to the children that the story can be recorded in the form of a story map. Look at the photocopiable page, which is a story map of Sleeping Beauty. Draw out from the children, the high points and low points in the story. Explain that the map dips when something unhappy or sad happens, but the line jumps up to a peak when an exciting or happy event takes place.

Once the children have understood the structure of the story map, they should then have a go at creating a simple story map of a familiar story, for example 'Little Red Riding Hood'. They can then apply the basic principle to devising story maps for chapters of novels, for short stories, or for complete novels.

A Story Map of Sleeping Beauty

The fairies were once asked to the christening of a baby princess.	One fairy was not invited, so she cast an evil spell on to the child. She said that on the girl's eighteenth birthday she would prick her finger on a spinning wheel and die.	However, a good fairy cast another spell to say that the princess would not die, but sleep for 100 years. She could only be awakened by a kiss.	The princess grew up to be beautiful and good.	On her 18th birthday, she went to a room high up in the castle and found an old lady spinning. (This was the bad fairy in disguise.) The princess touched the spindle and fell asleep.

Soon the whole palace fell asleep exactly where they were.	Time went by. The hedge around the palace grew thicker and thicker.	One day a handsome prince came riding by. He went to explore. He cut back the hedge and found the palace.	He went into the palace and found the room where the princess lay asleep.	He kissed her and immediately everyone inside the palace awoke after the long sleep. The prince and princess married and lived happily ever after.

A Story Map of

High Points | Start | Low Points

High Points | Start | Low Points

The Thirteenth Hour!

From Tom's Midnight Garden by Philippa Pearce

The grandfather clock was still there, anyway, and must tell him the true time. It must be either twelve or one: there was no hour between. There was no thirteenth hour.

Tom never reached the clock with his enquiry, and may be excused for forgetting on this occasion, to check its truthfulness. His attention was distracted by the opening of a door down the hall - the door of the ground floor front flat. A maid trotted out.
Tom had seen housemaids only in pictures but he recognised the white apron, cap and cuffs, and the black stockings. (He was not an expert in fashions, but the dress seemed to him to be rather long for her). She was carrying paper, kindling wood and a box of matches.

He only had a second in which to observe these things. Then he realised that he ought to take cover at once; and there was no cover to take. Since he must be seen, Tom determined to be the first to speak - to explain himself.

He did not feel afraid of the maid, as she came nearer, he saw that she was only a girl. To warn her of his presence without startling her, Tom gave a cough; but she did not seem to hear it. She came on. Tom moved forward into her line of vision: she looked at him, but looked through him too, as though he were not there. Tom's heart jumped in a way he did not understand. She was passing him.

"I say!" He protested loudly, but she paid not the slightest attention. She passed him, reached the front door of the ground floor flat, turned the door handle and went in. There was no bell - ringing or unlocking of the door.

Tom was left gaping; and meanwhile, his senses began to insist upon telling him of experiences even stranger than this encounter. His one bare foot was on cold flagstone, he knew; yet there was a contradictory softness and warmth to the flag stone. He looked down and saw that he was standing on a rug - a tiger skin rug. There were other rugs down the hall. His eyes now took in the whole of the hall - a hall that was different. No laundry box, no milk bottles, no travel posters on the walls. The walls were decorated with a rich variety of other objects instead: a tall Gothic barometer, a fan of peacock feathers, a huge engraving of a battle (hussars and horses and shot riddled banners) and many other pictures. There was a big dinner gong, with its wash-leathered gong stick hanging beside it. There was a large umbrella stand holding umbrellas and walking sticks, and a parasol and an air-gun and what looked like the parts of a fishing-rod. Along the wall projected a series of bracket-shelves, each table-high. They were of oak, except for one towards the middle of the hall, by the grand-father clock. That was of white marble, and it was piled high with glass cases of stuffed birds and animals. Enacted on its chilly surface were scenes of hot bloodshed: an owl clutched a mouse in its claws; a ferret looked up from the killing of its rabbit; in a case in the middle a red fox slunk along with a game fowl hanging from its jaws.

In all that crowded hall, the only object that Tom recognised was the grandfather clock. He moved towards it, not to read its face, but simply to touch it - to reassure himself that this at least was as he knew it.

His hand was nearly upon it, when he heard a little breath behind him that was the maid passing back the way she had come. For some reason, she did not seem to make as much sound as before. He heard her call only faintly; "I've lit the fire in the parlour."

She was making for the door through which she had first come, and, as Tom followed her with his eyes, he received a curious impression: she reached for the knob, and then she seemed to go. That was it exactly: she went, but not through the door. She simply thinned out, and went...

The Thirteenth Hour!

Teacher's Notes

National Literacy Strategy Year 5 Term I.

To write new scenes or characters into a story in the manner of the writer, maintaining consistency of character and style, using paragraphs to organise and develop detail.

Explain to the children that Tom is staying with his Uncle and Aunt in their flat in an old house. The grandfather clock which can be found in the hall does not appear to keep very good time, so Tom is driven to investigate whether the clock has actually struck thirteen, as he believes he has heard it do. Then, read aloud the photocopiable passage "The Thirteenth Hour!" from Tom's Midnight Garden by Philippa Pearce.

Let the children read the passage to themselves at least once more. Ask the children what they think has happened. Who do they think the maid is? Why can she not see Tom? How does the house change? From what era do the children think the furnishings come and why? What will happen next in the story? What may happen to Tom?

Now ask the children to imagine what happens next in the story. Their story should begin at the point in the extract when Tom sees the maid. Instead of becoming invisible, the Maid might become aware of Tom and have a conversation with him. The maid might then take Tom on an exploratory visit of the house and garden. The story will end when Tom (somehow) returns to the 20th century.

Talk this through with the children, encouraging them to write their new scene as though it is part of the original story. The children should be taken back to the photocopiable passage to look at the details that make the house essentially Victorian. What might they find in other rooms? What would definitely not be found in the house? (e.g. T.V. Computer, etc). The children should then use the writing frame provided to plan their story. For those children who struggle to find ideas there is a writing support sheet. When the children have planned carefully, they can then write the story in full, redrafting if time allows.

The Thirteenth Hour!

Writing Support Sheet

Name: ______________________ **Date:** ______________

Here are some words and ideas to help you. Can you add to these?

Setting

A large old Victorian home – lots of rooms – beautiful furniture – grandfather clock – coal fires – pictures – brass bedstead – rich garden – long flower beds – tall trees – swing – beautifully kept – a gardener.

Don't forget – no TV, computer, CD player or radio!

Characters

Tom

Nine or ten years old, excited or afraid, dressed in modern clothes.

Maid

Young girl wearing a long dark dress and apron, she is friendly, happy, wants to show Tom around. She knows all about the house and the family.

The Family

Mother

Long dark dress, hair in a bun.

Father

Tall, dark suit, moustache, stern.

Children

Girl Long dress and pinafore

Boy Wearing a suit with shorts and knee socks, and also a shirt and tie.

The Thirteenth Hour!

Writing Frame

Name: ______________________ **Date:** ____________

The story setting:

Characters in the story:

The story begins when Tom is spotted by the maid. What does she say? How does Tom react? What is she like?

Where does the maid take Tom to visit? What does he see?

Who does Tom meet?

How is the story resolved? How does he get back to the present?

All Alone in the World!

From The Secret Garden by Frances Hodgson Burnett

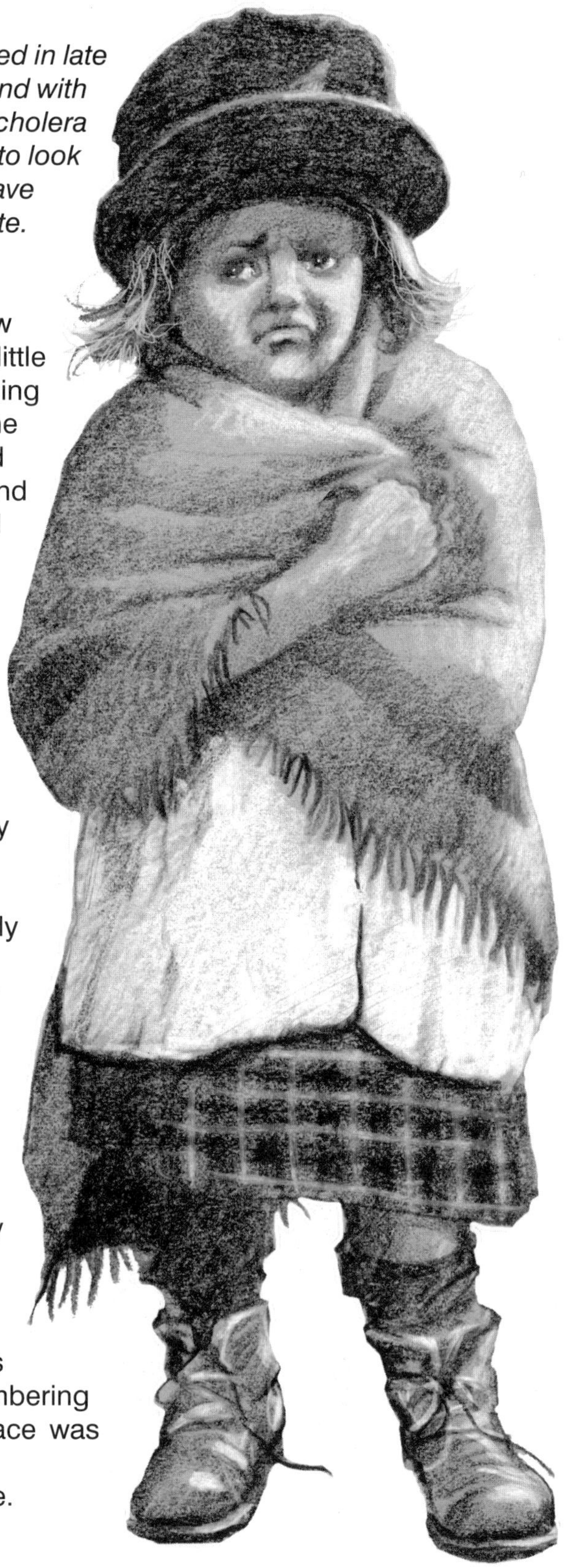

This is the story of a little girl Mary Lennox who lived in late Victorian times in India, surrounded by servants and with parents she hardly saw. A terrible disease called cholera has struck the household and Mary has been left to look after herself, unaware of the terrible events that have taken place. Two soldiers have come to investigate.

Mary was standing in the middle of the nursery when they opened the door a few minutes later. She looked an ugly, cross little thing and was frowning because she was beginning to be hungry and feel disgracefully neglected. The first man who came in was a large officer she had once seen talking to her father. He looked tired and troubled, but when he saw her he was so startled that he almost jumped back.

"Barney!" he cried out. "There is a child here! A child alone! In a place like this! Mercy on us, who is she?"

"I am Mary Lennox," the little girl said, drawing herself up stiffly. She thought the man was very rude to call her father's bungalow 'A place like this!' "I fell asleep when everyone had the cholera and I have only just wakened up. Why does nobody come?"

"It is the child no one ever saw!" exclaimed the man, turning to his companions. "She has actually been forgotten!"

"Why was I forgotten?" Mary said, stamping her foot."Why does nobody come?"

The young man whose name was Barney looked at her very sadly. Mary even thought she saw him wink his eyes as if to wink tears away.

"Poor little kid!" he said. "There is nobody left to come."

It was in that strange and sudden way that Mary found out that she had neither father nor mother left; that they had died and been carried away in the night, and that the few native servants who had not died also had left the house as quickly as they could get out of it, none of them even remembering that there was Missie Sahib. That was why the place was so quiet. It was true that there was no one in the bungalow but herself and the little rustling snake.

All Alone in the World!

Teacher's Notes

National Literacy Strategy Year 5 Term 1:

To write new scenes or characters into a story in the manner of the writer, maintaining consistency of character and style, using paragraphs to organise and develop detail.

Explain to the children that the passage is about a little girl called Mary Lennox. The child lived during Victorian times not in England but out in India. Her parents were wealthy and like other English families who lived there at that time, had servants to work around the house. Mary's nanny was an Indian lady. However, instead of calling her Nanny she had the Indian title of Ayah. Mary had spent very little time with her parents and had lived for the greater part of her time in the nursery. She was a bad tempered little girl who was used to ordering the servants about and getting her own way. Unfortunately the household had been struck down by the dreadful disease called cholera and everyone else had either died or fled from the house, in fear of catching it too. The photocopiable excerpt is taken from the part of the story when two soldiers come to investigate what is happening. The passage should be read aloud to the children.

After reading the passage, explain that Mary was then sent on a ship back to England. Ask the children to write about what they think happens next in the story. Where do they think the child might have been sent and with whom might she have to live now that her parents are dead? Is Mary happy in her new home? Does she make friends?
The children should try to write their stories in the character and style of the original passage. Remind the children that the story is set in Victorian times, so there would be no T.V., computers etc. The children should also try to develop the character of Mary from the information given in the photocopiable passage. There is a writing frame to aid planning and a writing support sheet for those children who struggle to find ideas.

All Alone in the World!

Writing Support Sheet

Name: ______________________________ **Date:** ________________

Here are some words and ideas to help you. Can you add to these?

Setting

Huge ship, long journey, storm, cabins and decks, weeks on board ship.

Large /small old house in the country/ town, lots/few rooms, beautiful/shabby furniture, pictures on the walls, a large/small garden, flowers/tall trees, a tree swing.

Characters

Mary:
bad tempered, Victorian darkly coloured dress, pale and thin, does not trust others easily, bossy, perhaps nine or ten years of age.

Perhaps Mary goes to live with an Aunt and Uncle:
cheerful/bad tempered, old/young, rich/poor, happy/unhappy to have Mary to stay.

Perhaps Mary might have cousins:
Younger/older than Mary, friendly/ nasty to Mary, fun/unkind, boys/girls. The children may be looked after by a nanny, or have a special teacher who lives with them called a governess.

All Alone in the World!

Writing Frame

Name: ________________________ **Date:** ____________

The story setting:

Characters in the story:

The story begins from the point at which Mary is sent back to England.
What is her journey like? How does she feel about what is happening to her?

Who meets Mary in England? Where is she taken? Describe the place.

Who does Mary meet in her new home? Does she make friends?

How is the story resolved? Is Mary happy in her new home?
Does she remain grumpy and bad tempered or does she change?

Breathless

Wilfrid Noyce

Heart aches,
Lungs pant
The dry air
Sorry, scant.
Legs lift
And why at all?
Loose drift,
Heavy fall.
Prod the snow
It's easiest way;
A flat step is holiday.
Look up,
The far stone
Is many miles
Far and alone.
Grind the breath
Once more and on;
Don't look up
Till journey's done.
Must look up,
Glasses are dim.
Wrench of hand
Is breathless limb.
Pause one step,
Breath swings back;
Swallow once,
Dry throat is slack.
Then on to the far stone;
Don't look up,
Count the steps done.
One step,
One heart-beat,
Stone no nearer
Dragging feet.
Heart aches,
Lungs pant
The dry air
Sorry, scant.

Breathless

Teacher's Notes

National Literacy Strategy Year 5 Term 1:

To convey feelings, reflections or moods in a poem through the careful choice of words and phrases.

Read aloud the poem 'Breathless' by Wilfred Noyce, at least twice. Talk about what is happening in the poem. Ask the children about the problems climbers have when climbing at high altitudes. Talk about the effectiveness of the short lines and phrases in getting over the feeling of breathlessness. The poem has only two or three syllables to a line. What is the effect of this? Does the poem rhyme? Again, what effect does this have when it is read aloud?

Ask the children about events they have taken part in which have involved a lot of physical effort to achieve a goal (for example - running a long distance race, climbing a mountain, swimming in a race). Use this experience as the basis for the children's own poems. Talk about the form of the poem, short lines and phrases with words omitted to give the effect of breathlessness. Suggest the children avoid making their poems rhyme, as it is a difficult thing do well. It is vital that the poem is read aloud by both Teacher and class group, in order to get over the atmosphere of the climb and the feelings and breathlessness of the climber.

It is useful to model a poem on the board, drawing from individual class member's ideas. The poem should then be read aloud together by the class. The class poem should then be erased from the board and the children should write their own poems, using their own ideas.

There is a writing support sheet for those children who struggle to come up with ideas or who have special needs.

Breathless

Writing Support Sheet

Name: ______________________ **Date:** ______________

Here are some words and ideas to help you. Can you add some more?
Don't forget – when you write your poem, to make sure the lines are short and set out like the ones in breathless! Don't try to make your poem rhyme.

A Race on Sports Day

Legs ache, breath short, pain in side, mouth dry, chest tight, finishing line miles away, feet sore, sweat dripping, never get there! Almost there, cheering, shouting.

A Swimming Race

Starter's gun, water splashing, eyes stinging, legs ache, cheering, clapping, shouting, waves all around, arms sore, breathless, end in sight, swallow water.

Climbing a Mountain

Legs aching, feet blistered, shoes heavy, summit(top of the mountain) far away, body heavy, face dripping with sweat, legs like stone, dragging steps, look upwards, never do it, getting nearer, breath short, gasping, thirsty, throat dry, almost at the top.

Who Am I?

He is a bar of dark chocolate,
A smooth black cat's coat,
An exotic fruit cocktail,
A silver Porsche disappearing into the distance.
He is a plate of caviar,
A blade on a knife,
A frothy cappuccino,
A piece of black silk.
He is a midnight alarm
A tiger disguised as a pussycat,
A jet plane,
A perfect day.

by Richard (age 10)

James Bond

She is a piece of smooth black velvet,
A coach and horses,
A rosy red apple,
A fairy tale,
She is a sunny day,
A cottage garden in summer,
A perfect English rose.

By Emma (age 10)

Snow White

Who Am I?

Teacher's Notes

National Literacy Strategy Y5 Term 1

To write metaphors from original ideas or from similes.

Read aloud, the two photocopiable poems at least twice. Did the children guess the identity of the people in each poem? Talk about simile and metaphor as forms of comparison, and explain the difference. For example the first line of Emma's poem would have been a simile if the word 'like' had been added, "She is like a piece of smooth black velvet". However, the line is metaphorical because it describes Snow White as actually being a piece of black velvet.
The children should then choose a famous person they admire or a famous character from a film or book. They should then think of metaphorical comparisons they can make. It helps to think of food/drink, methods of transport, animals, aspects of nature/weather, hobbies, time of the day as starting points for metaphors. The opening line of their poem should begin with "He is a/She is a......

The teacher should then model a poem together with the class, line by line. This is useful as the children's understanding will become much clearer as the difference between simile and metaphor are reinforced. When the class are happy with the poem they have composed together, (encourage them to improve their lines by adding adjectives and adverbs) then all read the poem aloud together. The poem should then be erased from the board and the children should begin to compose their own poem.

It may take one or two drafts to achieve a poem that they are satisfied with. With individual children's permission, it is a good follow up activity to read the poem aloud for the class to guess the famous person's identity. There is a writing support sheet for this activity, for children with special needs or those who find it a particularly difficult task.

Who Am I?

Writing Support Sheet

Name: ______________________________ **Date:** ________________

Here are some words and ideas to help you. Can you add to these? Don't forget to set out your poem like the 'Who Am I?' poems on the photocopiable sheet.

Count Dracula

An icicle, a winter's day, a starless night sky, a black marble gravestone, a poisonous plant, a sleek black hearse, a man - eating shark, a bitter cup of coffee.

Sleeping Beauty

A piece of cream cake, a vase of white roses, a white Rolls Royce, a Summer's day, a carefully wrapped birthday present, a perfect blue sky, the sound of birds singing.

Superman

A bright red sports car, a holiday in the sun, a Big Mac Meal, a race horse in action,
A flash of lightning, a Christmas surprise, an adventure story.

The Good Samaritan

Characters:
The Good Samaritan
Narrator
A Priest
A Levite
An Innkeeper

(A man is lying on the ground. He is obviously hurt and beaten.)

Narrator: A man was once travelling from Jerusalem to Jericho, when he was set upon by robbers and beaten up and left for dead. It so happened that a priest came by.

(Priest sees the wounded man, but keeps his distance from him.)

Priest: What a terrible shame! Robbers must have set upon that man. I would love to help him but I am clean and dressed up ready for the service in the temple. I really must dash I am late!

(The Priest walks past the man.)

Narrator: Next, along came a Levite.

Levite: Oh dear, he looks a mess. I'd better watch out, those robbers may still be lurking behind those rocks over there. I must go!

(The Levite walks past the man.)

Narrator: However, a man from Samaria, a Samaritan was also travelling that way. When he saw the poor victim lying there he felt sorry for the man and went over to help.

Samaritan: Oh good gracious, you are in a mess. Let me bandage your cuts and I'll take you to an Inn nearby. The Innkeeper is a kind man who will look after you.

Narrator: The Samaritan put the man on his donkey and took him to an Inn

Innkeeper: Oh dear, he's in a bit of a mess.

Samaritan: (To the Innkeeper) Please look after this man. Here is some money - if you need more then I will pay you when I return.

(The Samaritan leaves to continue about his business.)

The Good Samaritan

Part One

Teacher's Notes

National Literacy Strategy Y5 Term I:

Write own play script, applying conventions learned from reading, include production notes.

Read the script on the photocopiable page, using different children to read the parts. It would be useful to read this through at least twice and would also give more children the opportunity to read a part.

Talk about the conventions of script writing. For example, the list of characters at the beginning, production notes and stage directions in brackets. Then, discuss the meaning of the story. Explain that it is really a story about racial prejudice, as the Samaritans were the enemies of the Jews. Therefore the Samaritan would be expected to be the villain but actually was the person who showed kindness.

Talk about prejudice and the kinds of prejudice people have nowadays. Ask the children to get into small groups of 3 or 4 and to make up a short play about modern prejudice, in which the unexpected character becomes the helper or hero. The children should then write a play script for their short play about a 'Modern Good Samaritan'.

When these have been refined and practised, each group can perform it's play in front of the class. After each presentation, the children can together evaluate the script and performance for dramatic interest and Impact.

The Good Samaritan

Writing Support Sheet

Name: ______________________ **Date:** ______________

The Good Samaritan – (a modern version)

Characters

The Tramp . . . . .he is the good Samaritan who helps the boy.
Narrator . . . . .he tells the story.
Tom . . . . .the school boy who is attacked.
John and Chris . . . . .the boys who attack Tom.
Lady Felicity and Lord John . . . .walk on past the injured boy.

Narrator One day Tom went to the shop for his Mum. She had given him a £20 note. As he ran past carrying the money, two boys saw the £20 note. They decided to chase Tom and snatch it from him

John Let's run after that boy! ______________________

Chris Yes ______________________

(So they ran after Tom and caught him, beat him up and stole the £20 note. They ran away laughing. Poor Tom lay ______________________)

Narrator Then Lady Felicity and Lord John got out of their Rolls Royce and saw Tom lying there cut and bleeding. They did not want to help the boy

Lady Felicity ______________________

Lord John ______________________

Narrator Poor Tom lay there crying and in pain. Would no one help him? Then a tramp came past. He stopped, feeling very sorry for the boy and came over to help.

Tramp ______________________

Narrator The tramp took the boy to ______________________

Then he rang Tom's Mum so ______________________

The Good Samaritan

Writing Frame

Name: ______________________________ **Date:**__________________

An Evaluation of the Script and Performance of The Good Samaritan (a Modern Version) by ____________________________ Group.

A short explanation of the group's play explaining what it was about.

Was the story effective, lively and interesting? If so, why or if not, why not?

Which parts of the play did you most enjoy? Why?

Which actor or character was most dramatic, interesting, or lively from your point of view as one of the audience?

Was the play a dramatic success? Did the audience react well to the play as a whole? Were there aspects of the play or its production which, in your opinion should have been changed?

The Good Samaritan

Part Two

Teacher's Notes

National Literacy Strategy Y5 Term 1

To evaluate the script and the performance for their dramatic interest and impact.

Following the group performances of their Modern Versions of the Good Samaritan story, the children should discuss the dramatic impact and merits of each group's attempt. It is important to emphasise to them, the need for a positive approach as feelings can be easily hurt by thoughtlessly critical comments!

It is important that the children understand that criticism in this context should be both positive as well as negative. It would be useful to read short excerpts from newspaper reviews of theatre productions, as examples.

The children should choose the play that they most enjoyed and write a simple evaluation, using the writing frame.

The Good Samaritan

Writing Frame

Name: ______________________ **Date:** ______________

An Evaluation of the Script and Performance of The Good Samaritan (a Modern Version) by ______________________ Group.

The group's play was about: ______________________

____

____

I thought the play was good because: ______________________

____

____

The part of the play which I enjoyed most was when: ______________________

____

The reason I liked that part was: ______________________

____

The character I liked best was: ______________________

____

I thought that ____________ was good at acting the part because ____________

____

I think the group's play was successful because the audience seemed to:

____

In my opinion, one thing the group could have done to improve it's play was to:

____

Cinderella

Cinderella has been to the ball at the palace. As she was leaving, she was in a great hurry and left behind her slipper. The Prince, who had fallen in love with her, found the slipper and decided he would search until he had found the owner, as he had no other clue with whom he had been dancing. The Prince arrives at Cinders' house. Cinders is working away in the kitchen while her two ugly, lazy step-sisters are delighted by the arrival of the Prince.

Scene - The Kitchen

Characters

Buttons ....a poor boy who is Cinders' friend
The Prince ....the King's son
Gertie ....an ugly step-sister
Doris ....the second step-sister
The Prince's Servant ..always at the Prince's side
Cinders ....the beautiful but badly treated step-sister of Gertie and Doris
Baron ....Cinders' Father

Buttons Look, his Royal Highness the Prince.

Baron Your Highness.

Prince We are here on most urgent business, Baron. Are your daughters at home?
(GERTIE AND DORIS RUN ON FROM THE LEFT)

Gertie Princekins

Doris Princey

Prince Good morning ladies. Proceed servant.

Servant His Highness has decreed that every lady must try on this slipper. She whom it fits shall be his bride.

Gertie What a coincidence! I lost a slipper just like that one last night, didn't I Doris?

Doris Don't be silly, it was me.

Servant One minute, madam, this slipper must be fitted in his Highness's presence, so if you would just sit down.

(EACH OF THE STEP SISTERS TAKES A TURN AT TRYING ON THE SLIPPER)

Doris Anyone got a shoe horn? Nearly got it. That's it. It fits! It fits!

Servant Except for the heel.

Gertie Goody! Me next.
(GERTIE PUSHES DORIS OFF THE CHAIR)

Doris I don't know what you are in such a hurry for. If it didn't fit me, it certainly won't fit you!

Gertie I bet it does! I'll have you know I have a very short foot.

Servant Well, inches or centimetres, this particular foot is too long to go into this slipper.

(SERVANT TURNS AND SPEAKS TO THE PRINCE)
I'm sorry your Highness, the slipper doesn't fit either of these two 'ladies'. They're the last two in the land! The owner of the slipper does not exist.

Prince Don't be ridiculous! Of course she exists. I danced with her until midnight and then, just as the clock struck, she vanished leaving nothing behind but a slipper – and the memory of her lips on mine as we kissed! We must find her!

Gertie This is where it gets all sloppy and sentimental.

Doris I wish he would get all sloppy and sentimental with me!

Prince Let's go and check the list of all the people we invited to the ball once more. We might have missed someone! Lead the way to the list, hopefully for the last time.

ALL LEAVE. LAST ONE TO GO IS DORIS WHO PICKS UP THE SLIPPER AND HAS ONE FURTHER ATTEMPT TO FORCE IT ON. SHE FAILS AND WITH A SNORT OF DISGUST, FLINGS IT DOWN AND LEAVES THE STAGE.

(CINDERELLA ENTERS)

Cinders Oh just look at the state of this place! As usual it's left to me to clear up.

(CINDERELLA PICKS UP THE SLIPPER AND TRIES IT ON)

Cinders They've even left a pair of shoes here! No, I'm wrong, it's just one shoe or slipper rather. Actually it fits quite well, and it looks quite familiar too. I'm sure I've seen a pair like this somewhere before! Where was it now? There was music, I remember...

(CINDERELLA STARTS TO DANCE AROUND SINGING THE MUSIC TO THE DANCE. THE PRINCE AND HIS SERVANT ENTER)

Prince Well, that's it. We've checked the list and all are accounted for - except for that princess I danced with – and nobody knows who or where she is. So all we have is her memory and a slipper.

Servant We haven't even got the slipper. I left it just here and now that's gone as well!

(SERVANT TURNS TOWARDS CINDERELLA)

Oh, hello Cinders! I don't suppose you've seen a slipper lying around – Why! Your wearing it! Does it fit?

Cinders Yes! It's very comfortable – I wish I could find the other then I would have a pair just like those I dreamed about last night.

Prince What did you dream about?

Cinders I dreamed that I was at a ball – I had a lovely dress – I danced with the prince – and – and....

Prince Like this.

(THE PRINCE TAKES CINDERELLA IN HIS ARMS AND DANCES AROUND THE ROOM)

Cinders Ooh! Yes! Just like that. It made me feel like a princess.

Prince That's because it is real. You are a princess, my princess. Oh do say you'll marry me.

Cinders Oh yes! I will. But promise me one thing.

Prince My darling – anything! Just name it and it is yours.

Cinders Promise me you will buy me a pair of slippers exactly like those I wore in my dream, so that I can wear them at our wedding.

Prince Oh my dearest.

(THEY EMBRACE)

Prince Servant.

Servant Sire?

Prince Make all the arrangements for a royal wedding, with music and dancing and more food than anyone could imagine.

Servant With pleasure Sire.

Prince & Cinders The pleasure is all ours!

Cinderella

Teacher's Notes

National Literacy Strategy Year 5 Term 1:

To annotate a section of playscript as a preparation for performance, taking into account pace, movement, gesture and delivery of lines and the needs of the audience.

The photocopiable playscript is a short scene from the end of the pantomime Cinderella. For those children who are unfamiliar with the story of Cinderella it would be useful to read them a simple version of the story. (For example the ladybird version). It would also be useful to talk to the children about pantomime.

The script activity sheet would be best talked about together in a class discussion to ensure that the more technical dramatic terms are understood. The children could work in small groups to practise acting out the script. They could work together to annotate the script in the ways that the worksheet asks them to. This activity will be very difficult for those children who have reading problems. It would be useful for an adult to work alongside them, to help the children to read the lines. A small part like that of the Baron could be a useful way to include a child with severe reading difficulties ensuring they are not left out.

When the children have annotated their scripts and have practised performing it a sufficient number of times to feel confident, it would be fun to perform it for another class. Afterwards, it would be useful to try to evaluate the performance, to see if the script annotations were useful and consider what the children might change, a second time around.

Cinderella

Script Activity Sheet

Name: ______________________ **Date:** ______________

Read the script through at least twice, so that you know exactly what is happening in this scene. Then read the Explanation box below carefully, before attempting the activities below.

Explanation

Gesture: a movement of a part of your body to give special meaning to the lines being said or to express a feeling.

Movement: this is when actors have to move to a different part of the stage, as part of the action or story.

Delivery of lines: this is how the actor says the lines (For example, if the character is angry in the play, the actor would have to say the lines loudly or in a cross voice)

Audience response: This is how the audience reacts to what is happening on the stage. (For example, if there has just been a joke, then the audience will laugh. The actors will have to remember to wait till the audience is quiet again before saying their next line or it will not be heard.)

Pace: This is about making sure the play is lively and interesting.(For example, if the actors say their lines too slowly, or pause a lot between lines, then the play will become boring)

Now

1. Highlight in yellow on your script, all the places where you feel it is important that the actor uses a gesture.
2. Now think about movement. Read through the script and mark on it in red pen, when and where the characters move to. To save space and time, use letters instead of whole words. For example: S.R. = stage right, S.L.=stage left, M = middle. You can make up others of your own.
3. Now underline any of the character's lines which must be said in a special type of voice. Then, in brackets next to the lines say how the line should be said. For example, when Buttons sees the Prince he says, "*Look his Highness the Prince*" (excitedly)
4. Mark with a star, all the places where a character would have to pause, to wait for the audience to stop laughing.

When you have marked all these on your play-script then practise performing it to see if your ideas will work.

How the Whale Became

In the story, How The Whale Became by Ted Hughes, God finds a very strange object growing in his garden. God is baffled by the shiny black thing which just keeps on growing and growing until it is as long as the street! It has even demolished God's house in the process! All the creatures meet together with God to decide what should be done. Finally, they decide what must be done. This is how the story continues........

"Into the sea!" cried Mouse.
"No!"cried Whale-Wort.
"Into the sea!" cried all the creatures. And they hauled on the ropes. Whale-Wort's root came out of the ground. He began to thresh and twist, beating down houses and trees with his long root, as the creatures dragged him will-nilly through the countryside.
At last they got him to the top of a high cliff. With a great shout they rolled him over the edge and into the sea.
"Help!" cried Whale-Wort. "I shall drown! Please let me come back on land where I can sleep."
"Not until you're smaller!" shouted God. "Then you can come back."
"But how am I to get smaller?" wept Whale-Wort, as he rolled to and fro in the sea. "Please show me how to get smaller so that I can live on land."
God bent down from the high cliff and poked Whale-Wort on the top of his head with his finger.
"Ow!" cried Whale-Wort. "What was that for?"
"You've made a hole. The water will come in."
"No it won't," said God. "But some of you will come out. Now just you start blowing some of yourself out through that hole."
Whale-Wort blew, and a high jet of spray shot up out of the hole that God had made.
"Now go on blowing," said God.
Whale-Wort blew and blew. Soon he was quite a bit smaller. As he shrank, his skin, that had been so tight and glossy, became covered with tiny wrinkles.
At last God said to him:
"When you're as small as a cucumber, just give a shout. Then you can come back into my garden. But until then, you shall stay in the sea."
And God walked away with all his creatures, leaving Whale-Wort rolling and blowing in the sea.
Soon Whale-Wort was down to the size of a bus. But blowing was hard work, and by this time he felt like a sleep. He took a deep breath and sank down to the bottom of the sea for a sleep. Above all, he loved to sleep.
When he awoke he gave a roar of dismay. While he was asleep he had grown back to the length of a street and the fatness of a ship with two funnels.
He rose to the surface as fast as he could and began to blow. Soon he was back down to the size of a lorry.
But soon, too, he felt like another sleep. He took a deep breath and sank to the bottom.
When he awoke he was back to the length of a street.
This went on for years. It is still going on.

As fast as Whale-Wort shrinks with blowing, he grows with sleeping. Sometimes, when he is feeling very strong, he gets himself down to the size of a motor-car. But always, before he gets himself down to the size of a cucumber, he remembers how nice it is to sleep. When he wakes, he has grown again.
He longs to come back on land and sleep in the sun, with his root in the earth. But instead of that, he must roll and blow, out in the wild sea. And until he is allowed to come back on land, the creatures call him just Whale.

From 'How the Whale Became and Other Stories' by Ted Hughes

How the Whale Became

Teacher's Notes

The National Literacy Strategy Y5 Term : 2

To write own versions of legends, myths and fables using structures and themes identified in reading.

Read aloud the photocopiable abridged version of the story 'How the Whale Became' by Ted Hughes, or the whole of the story if a copy is available. Ask the children to read it again to themselves. Question the children on the narrative structure to ensure they have understood the sequence of events in the story.

Then begin to think about other animals with which they are familiar, e.g. pets, wild animals, zoo animals and together make up stories orally to explain how they gained their particular characteristics. For example, the rabbit may have gained his long ears because he was so nosy, he was always listening in to other creatures conversations. One day, he was so busy listening in that he hadn't noticed, a prickly gorse bush. His fur was stuck in the gorse and he had to pull and pull to free his ears. The result was that rabbit was left with ears as long as they are today.

The children should share lots of ideas and stories orally, prior to writing down the story title of how their creature gained its particular features. This will be of great help to those children who struggle to think up ideas of their own. The title of their story could be 'How the..........became..........'

There is a writing frame for the children to use at the planning stage. For the children who struggle to find ideas or who have special needs, there is a writing support sheet. When the children have completed the planning, they should write the story in full. The final versions could be put into a class anthology of writing entitled, 'How the Creatures Became'.

How the Whale Became

Writing Support Sheet

Name: ______________________ **Date:** ______________

Here are some ideas to help you. Can you think of some more of your own?

How the Mouse Became

Mouse was a nosy creature who enjoyed listening in on other people's conversations and pretending afterwards that he hadn't done this at all.
Other creatures set a trap for him. He almost gets away but is caught by his tail. He pulls and pulls and at last gets away but is left with a long tail.

How the Lion Got His Mane

There were once two lion cubs, Tika (a girl) and Bruno (a boy). Their mother warned them not to go near the fuzzy wuzzy bush. If you did the sticky fuzzy wuzzies would stick all over you and never come off.
Tika obeyed her mother. Bruno was more adventurous. He didn't believe his mother's story, and went to see for himself. Well you can guess what happened- the fuzzy wuzzies stuck to his head! No matter how much he rolled around they would not come off. That is how the lion got is mane.

How the Giraffe Became

Giraffe was very greedy. He loved the leaves from the bushes and the fresh green ones on the tall trees.
One day he felt really hungry when he saw the most juicy leaves at the top of the tall tree. He decided to climb up. He had long legs so this was not easy.
He stretched his head as far as he dared to the highest part of the tree but he slipped. Soon he was holding on to the branch by his teeth and his legs were dangling. As time went on his neck began to stretch with the weight of his body and legs. After he got down from the tree his neck stayed as long as it is today.

How the Whale Became

Writing Frame

Name: ______________________________ **Date:** ____________________

The story setting:

The characters/creatures involved in the story:

In the opening paragraph, the creature you have chosen is introduced.

What happens to the creature so that it gains its own particular characteristics?

How is the situation resolved? Does he/she live happily now? Do other creatures accept or reject the changes?

Chivvy

by Michael Rosen (From You Tell Me, Poems by Roger McGough and Michael Rosen)

Grown-ups say things like:
Speak up.
Don't talk with your mouth full
Don't stare
Don't point
Don't pick you nose
Sit up
Say please
Less noise
Shut the door behind you
Don't drag your feet
Haven't you got a hankie?
Take your hand out of your pockets
Pull your socks up
Stand up straight
Say thank you
Don't interrupt
No one thinks you're funny
Take your elbows off the table
Can't you make up your own
mind up about anything?

Chivvy

Teacher's Notes

The National Literacy Strategy Y5 T2:

To use the structures of poems read to write extensions based on these, e.g. additional verses, or substituting own words and ideas.

Read aloud the poem 'Chivvy' by Michael Rosen, to the class. Then read it aloud all together. Ask the children about the ideas in the poem. Are some of these comments familiar to them? What sort of things do the children's parents complain about?

Give the children a choice of people to write their poems about. For example their poem could be about things that teachers or dinner ladies say to them. Their title might be- 'Teachers Say Things Like...' or 'Dinner Ladies Say Things Like...'. Then get the children to brainstorm ideas on their chosen title. There is a writing support sheet for those children who struggle to come up with ideas. It would be useful to share some of the ideas that the children have come up with. Then talk about the form of Rosen's poem – bringing out the idea that it does not rhyme and that each line is short and begins with a capital letter.

Using the children's ideas model a poem on the board. Read it aloud together and then erase the poem. The children should then write their own poem using the brainstormed ideas. When final drafts are completed the children could read them aloud. The poems could be included in a class anthology.

Chivvy

Writing Support Sheet

Name: ____________________ **Date:** ____________

Here are some ideas to help you. Can you think of some more?

Teachers say things like:

Work in Silence. Who do you think you are talking to? I'm waiting. Please listen. Sit up and behave yourself. I'll have to speak to your mother. Don't interrupt. The whole class is waiting. This work won't do, STAY IN AT PLAYTIME.

Dinner Ladies say things like:

Don't talk with your mouth full. Say thank you. Don't burp, its rude. EAT UP! Your Mum's spent good money on that. Chew what you're eating. Don't say you don't like it. Queue quietly. Stop messing about. I'll tell your teacher about you.

The Birth of Jesus

At that time the Emperor Augustus ordered a census to be taken through-out the Roman Empire. When this first census took place, Quirinius was the governor of Syria. Everyone, then went to register himself, each to his own town.
Joseph went from the town of Nazareth in Galilee to the town of Bethlehem in Judea, the birthplace of King David.

Joseph went there because he was a descendant of David. He went to register with Mary, who was promised in marriage to him. She was pregnant and while they were in Bethlehem, the time came for her to have her baby. She gave birth to her first son, wrapped him in strips of cloth and laid him in a manger - there was no room for them to stay in the inn.

The Shepherds and the Angels

There were some shepherds in that part of the country who were spending the night in the fields, taking care of their flocks. An angel of the Lord appeared to them, and the glory of the Lord shone over them. They were terribly afraid, but the angel said to them. Don't be afraid! I am here with good news for you, which will bring great joy to all the people. This very day in David's town your Saviour was born - Christ the Lord! And this is what will prove it to you: you will find a baby wrapped in strips of cloth and lying in a manger.

Suddenly a great army of heaven's angels appeared with the angel, singing praises to God: Glory to God in the highest heaven, and peace on earth to those with whom he is pleased!

When the angels went away from them back into heaven, the shepherds said to one another, "Let's go to Bethlehem and

see this thing that has happened, which the Lord has told us."
So they hurried off and found Mary and Joseph and saw the baby lying in the manger. When the shepherds saw him, they told them what the angel had said about the child. All who heard it were amazed at what the shepherds said. Mary remembered all these things and thought deeply about them. The shepherds went back, singing praises to God for all they had heard and seen; it had been just as the angel had told them.

(Luke Ch 2)

Visitors from the East

Jesus was born in the town of Bethlehem in Judea, during the time when Herod was king. Soon afterwards, some men who studied the stars came from the east to Jerusalem and asked, "Where is the baby born to be the King of the Jews? We saw his star when it came up in the east, and we have come to worship him."

When King Herod heard about this he was very upset, and so was everyone else in Jerusalem. He called together all the chief priests and the teachers of the Law and asked them. "Where will the Messiah be born?"

In the town of Bethlehem in Judaea they answered. For this is what the prophet wrote: Bethlehem in the land of Judah, you are by no means the least of the leading cities of Judah; for from you will come a leader who will guide my people Israel.

So Herod called the visitors from the east to a secret meeting and found out from them the exact time the star had appeared. Then he sent them to Bethlehem with these instructions: "Go and make a careful search for the child, and when you find him, let me know, so that I too may go and worship him."

And so they left, and on their way they saw the same star they had seen in the east. When they saw it, how happy they were, what joy was theirs! It went ahead of them until it stopped over the place where the child was. They went into the house, and when they saw the child with his mother Mary, they knelt down and worshipped him. They brought out their gifts of gold, frankincense, and myrrh, and presented them to him.

Then they returned to their country by another road, since God had warned them in a dream not to go back to Herod.

The Escape to Egypt

After they had left, an angel of the Lord appeared in a dream to Joseph and said, "Herod will be looking for the child in order to kill him. So get up, take the child and his mother and escape to Egypt, and stay there until I tell you to leave."
Joseph got up, took the child and his mother, and left during the night for Egypt, where he stayed until Herod died. This was done to make what the Lord had said through the prophet come true, "I called my Son out of Egypt."

(Matthew Ch 2)

The Birth of Jesus

Teacher's Notes

The National Literacy Strategy Y5 Term2:

To review and edit writing to produce a final form, matched to the needs of an identified reader.
(This activity, although in Y5 Term 2 section of The National Literacy Strategy, I would swap with one of the later activities from Y5 T1.It is obviously a Christmas Activity and is one which I have used over and over again with the children and both writer and audience have taken delight in the end product. I feel it is justifiable to therefore use it in Term1.)

Read aloud to the children, the Nativity Story excerpts found on the photocopiable pages, several times, until the events of the Christmas Story are very familiar. It may be useful to make a simple story map of the events prior to beginning the activity.

The children should then begin to explore the idea of making a Nativity Story book for a Reception or Y1 class. It is a useful activity to gather together some favourite books of the Reception/Y1 class and to take time for the children to examine the kind of material which is both appropriate and enjoyable for 5 & 6 year olds. Make up a guideline with the children of the sort of factors they need to take into consideration when putting together their Nativity Story (e.g. amount of text, size of print, number of words on a page, type of vocabulary used, ratio of picture to text, appealing front cover, etc.)

The children should then begin to decide on an appropriate number of pages for their book and what might be included on each page. This can be planned out in rough, with suggestions for appropriate illustrations that might be used, on each page. Once a plan for the book is made, the children can then devise a title page and write the text out in full. It is useful at this stage for the children to review and edit their stories in a small group. The children can positively criticise their rough draft suggesting ways in which the vocabulary, etc. might be improved.

When the final text is agreed on, and is felt to be appropriate for an audience of Reception/Y1, then the children should begin to make their books. If time allows these could be linked into Design Technology or Art time. Some pop-ups could be made or specific techniques used for the art work. It is important that enough books are made, so that each of the Reception/Y1 children receive a book to take home as a special Christmas present. It is a good idea for each child to take their finished book to the Infant Children to share reading it with them. I have found that both KS2 children and the infants derive a great deal from this activity.

There is a writing support sheet for those children who struggle with the sequence of ideas in this activity.

The Birth of Jesus

Writing Support Sheet

Name: ______________________________ **Date:** ____________________

Here are the events of the story and some words to help you.

Joseph went with Mary to Bethlehem to register his name.

Mary and Joseph found there was no room at the Inn. They slept in the barn. Jesus was born. He was put in a manger to sleep.

The Angels told the shepherds the Good news of Jesus' birth. They went to visit him. Some wise men, who studied the stars, went to Jerusalem to ask Herod where Jesus had been born. Herod was cross at the idea of another king being born. He asked the wise men to come back and tell him where Jesus was.

The wise men followed the star and found baby Jesus. They gave him gifts of gold, frankincense and myrrh. They did not go back to Herod but went back to their country another way.

An angel appeared to Mary and Joseph, warning that Herod wanted to kill Jesus so at night the family secretly went back to Egypt where they would be safe.

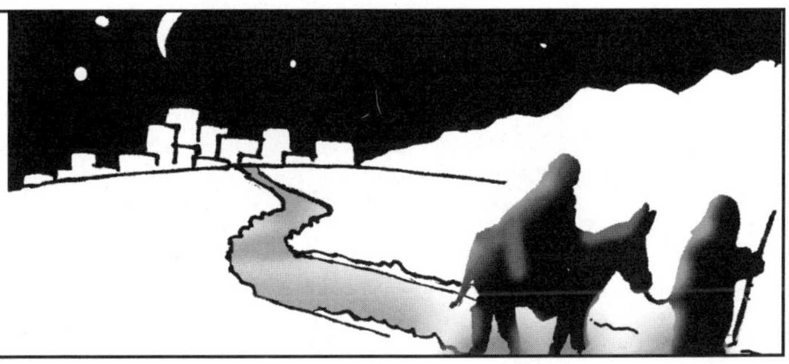

Moses the Kitten

by James Herriot

I went over and looked closer. It was a tiny kitten, probably about six weeks old, huddled and immobile, eyes tightly closed. Bending down, I poked gently at the furry body. It must be dead; a morsel like this couldn't possibly survive in such cold .... but no, there was a spark of life because the mouth opened soundlessly for a second then closed.

Quickly I lifted the little creature and tucked it inside my coat. As I drove into the farmyard I called to the farmer who was carrying two buckets out of the calf house.
"I've got one of your kittens here, Mr Butler. It must have strayed outside."

Mr Butler put down his buckets and looked blank. "Kitten? We haven't got no kittens at present."
I showed him my find and he looked more puzzled.
"Well, that's a rum 'un, there's no black cats on this spot. We've all sorts o' colours but no black 'uns."
"Well he must have come from somewhere else," I said. "Though I can't imagine anything so small travelling very far. It's rather mysterious."

I held the kitten out and he engulfed it with his
big, work-roughened hand.
"Poor little beggar, he's only just alive. I'll take him into t'house and see if the missus can do owt for him."

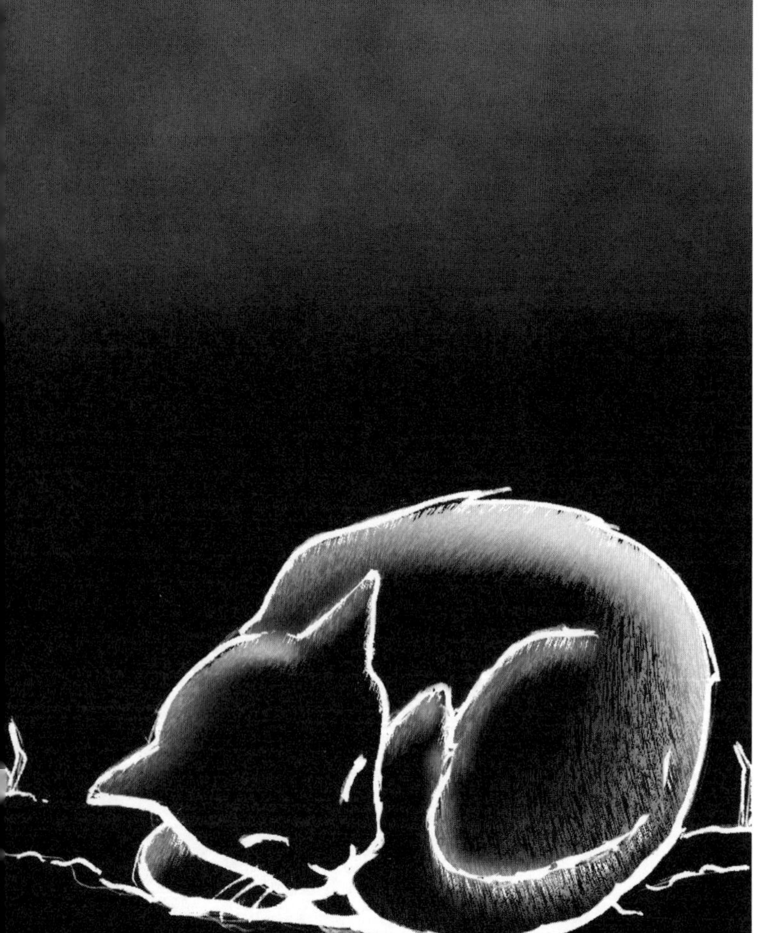

Moses the Kitten

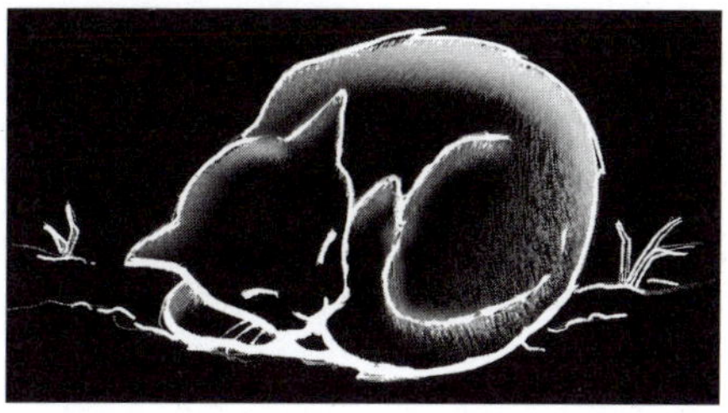

Teacher's Notes

The National Literacy Strategy Year 5 T3;

To write from another character's point of view, e.g. re-telling an incident in letter form.

Ask the children if any of them have read or heard of any James Herriot vet stories. Explain that he was a vet in a country practice and dealt with both farm animals and pets. Then, read the passage from the story on the photocopiable page at least twice. After reading the passage, discuss with the children their ideas of how the kitten came to be there. What had happened to him? Where he had come from? Then go on to talk about how the farmer's wife might have cared for Moses and whether or not he survived. If he did survive, did the farmer decide to keep the kitten and did it remain on the farm for the rest of its life or did it go elsewhere, perhaps to another farm or family.

The children should be asked to imagine they are one of the farmer's children. They should write a letter to a friend or relative explaining how and where Moses was found and how their mother took care of the kitten. Finally they might explain what happened to the kitten. Did it survive and if it did, was it kept on the farm or was it sent away to live elsewhere.

There is a writing frame to aid the children's planning. It will be necessary to go over the format for writing a letter. This could be modelled on the board prior to the children beginning their written work. There is also a writing support sheet for those children who have special needs or who struggle with this activity.

Moses the Kitten

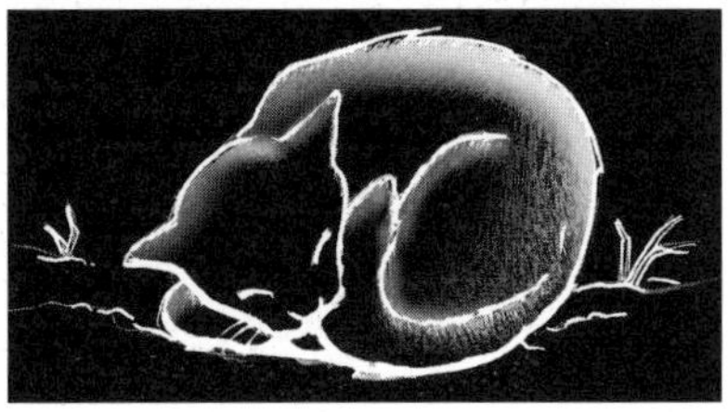

Writing Support Sheet

Name: ______________________ **Date:** ____________

Sunnyside Farm,
Lang Lane,
Chipping,
Yorkshire.
YO1 2BX
14th ________ 2001

Dear _________,

I hope you are feeling well. How is

Our vet, Mr Herriot found a kitten

He brought it to our farm to show my Dad because he thought it was ours. My Dad took it to my Mum.

We are lucky because Dad said we could have the kitten. I felt

I hope you and your family have a lovely

With love from,

____

Moses the Kitten

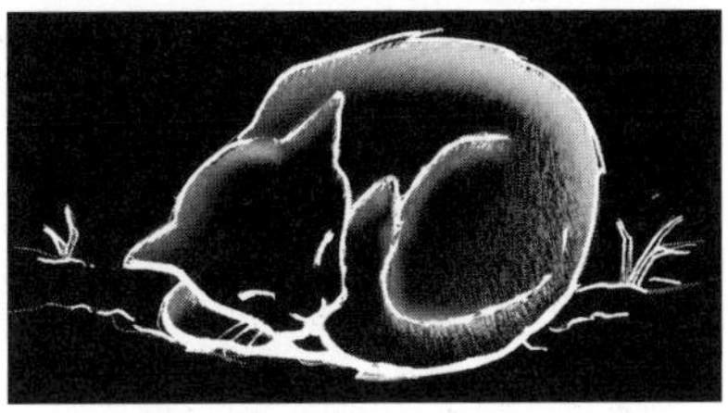

Writing Frame

Name: ______________________ **Date:** ______________

Farm Name
Address

Date

Dear

Begin the letter with a few lines in which you ask about the friend or relative and their family.

Tell of how Mr Herriot found the kitten and brought it to the farm.

How did your mother take care of the kitten? What has happened to it now?

End the letter politely again asking something about your friend's family and saying you hope to see him/her soon.

With love from,

Your signature

Reading Reflection Sheet

(For use whilst reading a book)

Teacher's Notes

The National Literacy Strategy Y5 T3:

To record predictions, questions, reflections while reading, e.g. through the use of a reading journal.

It is useful for the children to think about the book they have chosen to read with particular reference to content, characters, story events and prediction of what will happen next.

The children can complete the sheet and then talk about their chosen novel with others in a small group, or in a large class discussion. This helps them to clarify and express their views. These Reading Reflection Sheets could be put in a class file/book which all children have access to. These simple reviews might encourage other children to try the novel themselves and perhaps discourage children from becoming too "author bound."

There is a writing support sheet for those children who have special needs or who struggle with this activity.

Reading Reflection Sheet

Writing Support Sheet

Name: ______________________ **Date:** ______________

The book I am reading is ______________________

by ______________________

This is what has happened in the story so far. ______________________

The character I liked best was ______________________

I liked ______________________ because

The character I liked least was ______________________

I liked ______________________ least because

The most exciting part of the story was ______________________

I enjoyed this because ______________________

This is what I think will next happen in the story. ______________________

Reading Reflection Sheet

Writing Frame

Name: ______________________________ **Date:** ______________

Book Title.. ....

Author ....Illustrator ....

What has happened in the story so far:

The character I like best/least and why I like him/her best/least:

The most interesting/exciting/funny event in the story so far:

What I think will happen next:

Please, Sir, I want some More

From Oliver Twist by Charles Dickens

Oliver Twist and his companions suffered the tortures of slow starvation for three months: at last they got so voracious and wild with hunger, that one boy, who was tall for his age, and hadn't been used to that sort of thing (for his father had kept a small cookshop), hinted darkly to his companions, that unless he had another basin of gruel *per diem*, he was afraid he might some night happen to eat the boy who slept next to him, who happened to be a weakly youth of tender age. He had a wild, hungry eye; and they implicitly believed him. A council was held; lots were cast who should walk up to the master after supper that evening, and ask for more; and it fell to Oliver Twist.

The evening arrived; the boys took their places. The master, in his cook's uniform, stationed himself at the copper; his pauper assistants ranged themselves behind him; the gruel was served out; and a long grace was said over the short commons. The gruel disappeared; the boys whispered to each other, and winked at Oliver, while his next neighbours nudged him. Child as he was, he was desperate with hunger, and reckless with misery. He rose from the table, and advancing to the master, basin and spoon in hand, said: somewhat alarmed at his own temerity:
"Please, sir, I want some more."

The master was a fat, healthy man; but he turned very pale. He gazed in stupefied astonishment on the small rebel for some seconds, and then clung for support to the copper. The assistants were paralysed with wonder; the boys with fear.
'What!' said the master at length, in a faint voice.
"Please, sir," replied Oliver, "I want some more."

The master aimed a blow at Oliver's head with the ladle, pinioned him in his arms, and shrieked aloud for the beadle.

The board were sitting in solemn conclave, when Mr Bumble rushed into the room in great excitement, and addressing the gentleman in the high chair, said,
"Mr Limbkins, I beg your pardon, sir! Oliver Twist has asked for more!" There was a general start. Horror was depicted on every countenance.
"For more!" said Mr Limbkins. "Compose yourself, Bumble, and answer me distinctly. Do I understand that he has asked for more, after he had eaten the supper allotted by the dietary?"
"He did, sir," replied Bumble.

"That boy will be hung," said the gentleman in the white wasitcat; "I know that boy will be hung."
Nobody controverted the prophetic gentleman's opinion. An animated discussion took place. Oliver was ordered into instant confinement; and a bill was next morning pasted on the outside of the gate, offering a reward of five pounds to anybody who would take Oliver Twist off the hands of the parish. In other words, five pounds and Oliver Twist were offered to any man or woman who wanted an apprentice to any trade, business, or calling.

Please, Sir, I want some More

Teacher's Notes

National Literacy Strategy Year 5 Term 3:

To write in the style of the author, e.g. writing on to complete a section, resolve a conflict, writing additional dialogue, a new chapter.

Read the passage aloud to the children at least twice. Ask the children how the language of the passage compares to any other modern story they have read. Bring out the idea that the book was written over a hundred years ago and that is why some of the language sounds strange. Ensure that the children have understood clearly the events of the passage. They will need to know that Oliver Twist was an orphan. Some of the children will be familiar with the story, others will not. Talk about being an orphan in Victorian times and what life in an orphanage would have been like.

Collect words and phrases from the passage which indicate that it is not set in modern times.

The children should then be asked how they imagine the story might have continued from the point at which Oliver asks for more and he is advertised as an apprentice. (It is important that the children understand the meaning of this term). Who might take Oliver on – a baker, a butcher, a butler or as a servant in a wealthy mansion etc? Are they kind to Oliver? Is he happy/unhappy. Does he stay or run away again? There is a writing frame to aid the children's planning, and a writing support sheet to help those children that struggle with this activity.

It is important to emphasise to the children that they are writing in the third person, in the past tense. They should be encouraged to write in the style of Dickens trying to use some of the vocabulary and style of speech used in the photocopiable text.

Please, Sir, I want some More

Writing Support Sheet

Name: ______________________________ **Date:** ____________________

Here are some ideas to help you. Can you add to these ?

Setting

Orphanage- cold, dark, dull, painted in dark colours, hard chairs, uncomfortable beds
Poor orphan boys- thin, starving, scruffily dressed, no shoes or socks.
Oliver's new place of work – PERHAPS
1. A baker's shop – huge ovens, enormous bags of flour to carry, smell of baking bread, bakers in white aprons, working from four in the morning, long days at work.
OR
2.A mansion of a fine gentleman – open fires to clean out, coal to carry, floors to scrub, vegetables to prepare, serving at the table at important dinners, carrying trays of drinks to the master's friends, working long hours.

Characters

Mr. Bumble-bad tempered, stern, hard hearted man, dislikes boys, dressed in black.

Oliver- young lad of about ten years of age, brave, dressed in rags, hungry, cold unhappy, without anyone to love and take care of him.

New Master - MIGHT BE - kind, caring, fair, jolly, might take to Oliver and give him warm clothes, shoes, and plenty of good food.
OR MIGHT BE - nasty, unkind, mean, work poor Oliver very hard, expect him to get up early in the morning and work late at night, with little food.

Old Fashioned Language

Here are some words and phrases that you might include in your story-
Gruel (porridge), The master shrieked aloud (the master shouted aloud),
The boy's countenance (the boy's face), a bill was posted outside the gate (a poster was put up outside the gate), Oliver addressed his Master (Oliver spoke to his Master).

Please, Sir, I want some More

Writing Frame

Name: ______________________________ **Date:** ____________________

The story setting: (Think about the orphanage and where you imagine Oliver goes to work later.)
Characters in the story:
The story begins from the point at which Oliver asks for more and Mr Bumble puts up an advertisement outside the orphanage to find Oliver a place of work. Who takes him on and where does Oliver end up?
Describe his new home. Who does Oliver meet there?
What happens at his new place of work? Describe some of the things that happen to him. Is he happy / unhappy?
How is the story resolved? Does Oliver settle down or does he run away? Is he returned to the orphanage?

A Book Review

Teacher's Notes

National Literacy Strategy Year 5 Term 3:

To write discursively about a novel or story, e.g. to describe, explain or comment on it.

Begin by having a class discussion around the theme 'My Favourite Book'. Ask the children to orally summarise the plot of the story in a few sentences. Go on to talk about the characters the children liked best and why they like them. Discuss what were the high points in the plot. Were there particular moments which were very exciting or funny? Was the book illustrated and if so were the pictures appealing and did they add to the story?

Finally discuss who the children would recommend the book for. Consider age group, children with an interest in a type of genre, etc.
The children should then use the photocopiable Book Review Writing Frame, and then write the review in full. It would be interesting to follow this by reading a selection of reviews and encouraging children to swap novels to read at home. A class book of these reviews would be a really useful resource of all the children to dip into, prior to choosing reading material. It may be useful for encouraging reluctant readers to try a new genre.

A Book Review

Writing Support Sheet

Name: ______________________ **Date:** ______________

A book review of ______________________

by ______________________

This is what happened in the story ______________________

My favourite character was ______________________ because

The part of the story I enjoyed most was ______________________

The part of the story I enjoyed least was ______________________

I would recommend this book to a child of ________ years old, because

The book would be suitable for children who enjoy ______________________ genre.

A Book Review

Writing Frame

Name: ______________________________ **Date:** ______________

A Book Review of.. ....

by ....

Illustrated by ....

Summarise the story in this paragraph. Avoid making it any longer than 6 sentences. You could also mention if the book is illustrated and if you feel this helps the story.

____

____

____

____

Choose one or two favourite characters - describe them and say why they appeal to you and why you identify with them.

____

____

____

____

In your own words, relate the parts of the story you found most exciting or funny or sad. Try to say why you chose each part.

____

____

____

____

To whom would you recommend this book? Think about age range and whether it might be enjoyed by a girl or boy. Think about whether it would it be suitable for children who enjoy a particular genre. e.g. science fiction or historical stories.

____

____

____

____

Witches' Song

William Shakespeare

1st Witch Thrice the brinded cat hath mew'd

2nd Witch Thrice, and once the hedge-pig whin'd.

3rd Witch Harpier cries: 'tis time, 'tis time.

1st Witch Round about the cauldron go;
In the poison'd entrails throw.
Toad, that under cold stone
Days and nights has thirty one
Swelter'd venom sleeping got
Boil thou first i' the charmed pot.

All Double, double toil and trouble;
Fire burn, and cauldron bubble.

2nd Witch Fillet of a fenny snake,
In the cauldron boil and bake;
Eye of newt and toe of frog,
Wool of bat and tongue of dog,
Adder's fork and blind-worm's sting, Lizard's leg and howlet's wing,
For a charm of powerful trouble,
Like a hell-broth boil and bubble.

All Double, double toil and trouble;
Fire burn, and cauldron bubble.

3rd Witch Scale of dragon, tooth of wolf,
Witches' mummy, maw and gulf
Of the ravin'd salt-sea shark,
Root of hemlock digg'd i' the dark,
Liver of blaspheming Jew,
Gall of goat, and slips of yew
Silver'd in the moon's eclipse
Nose of Turk and Tartar's lips,
Add thereto a tiger's chaudron,
For the ingredients of a our cauldron.

All Double, double toil and trouble;
Fire burn, and cauldron bubble.

2nd Witch Cool it with a baboon's blood,
Then the charm is firm and good.

Witches' Song

Teacher's Notes

National Literacy Strategy Y5 T3:

To use performance poems as models to write and to produce poetry in polished forms through revising, redrafting and presentation.

Explain to the children that this poem is part of a play by Shakespeare 'Macbeth' which was written about two hundred and fifty years ago. Explain that written and spoken language does not stay the same and that when the children hear the poem, they will not understand every word. They should not attempt to understand every word but should appreciate the mood and atmosphere created by the language.

The poem should be read aloud, firstly by the teacher. (Try to read it in as witch like/evil a voice as possible, creating an atmosphere). The class should then read it aloud, as a piece of choral speaking. (The class could be divided into groups - a group as First Witch, Second Witch and Third Witch with everyone coming in on 'Double, double'. The teacher should then ask the class what they believe to be happening here. Explain that the witches are creating a wicked spell so that Macbeth can become King. Talk about some of the contents of the witches' cauldron (don't get too tied up with a translation of every word). Talk about the form of the poem - the fact that it rhymes and has a definite rhythm scheme (tap out the rhythm you will find there are mainly seven syllables in each line).

Explain that the spell need not have been to achieve something evil but could be to succeed in bringing goodness to the world. Talk about what a good spell might be trying to do. (e.g. bring peace, food for all, kindness, etc.) This would obviously change the type of ingredients that went into the cauldron.

The children should then choose a spell to do evil (get rid of school, homework, etc.) or one to do good. The children should write their own witches' song in the style of Shakespeare - try to achieve 7 beats in a line but it would be better if it did not rhyme as this is a very skilled form of writing. The opening line should keep the structure:

"Round about the cauldron go,"

and the Chorus lines

"Double, double toil and trouble
Fire burn, and cauldron bubble,"

should also be retained. The photocopiable pages which follow can be used for the children's final drafts. These poems should be reworked over a series of lessons, culminating in a class poetry reading session. The poems could be put together in a 'Book of Spells'. There is a writing support sheet for those children who struggle with this activity.

Witches' Song

Writing Support Sheet

Name: ______________________________ **Date:** ______________

Spells to do Good and Evil

Here are some words and ideas to help you. Can you think of some more?

Evil Spell

A spell to get rid of my teacher , the school, or homework.

Horrid objects to put in your cauldron- warts, spots, contents of the bin, ugly bugs, smelly socks, rotten eggs, stale bread, sour milk, black teeth, yellow scabs, dirty toe-nails.

Good Spell

A spell to make all wars end, enough food for the world, to make everyone happy.

Good objects to put in your cauldron- angels wings, the smell of roses, a baby's breath, a summer's day, a happy song, a laughing sound, a wish, a Christmas present, a bar of chocolate

Witches' Song

An *evil* spell to make ______________________

Round about the cauldron go ;
In these hideous objects throw.

Double, double toil and trouble;
Fire burn and cauldron bubble.

Witches' Song

A **good** spell to make ____________________

Round about the cauldron go;
In these wondrous objects throw!

Double, double fun and laughter;
I'll make good for ever after!